Thanks for the Lemonade

A 30-Day Devotional

True Story By Mary E. Rudisaile

Copyright 2020 by Mary E. Rudisaile

Written and Edited by Mary E. Rudisaile
Book Design by Makala James

All rights reserved. No part of these stories may be reproduced in any form without permission in writing from the author or copyright owner.

All Bible texts in this book are from The New King James Version. Copyright © 1979, 1980, 1982, by Thomas Nelson, Inc.

Printed in the United States of America.

First Printing, June 2020

ISBN: 9781707597581

Dedication

For Ty, Lee, Lori, Joe, Daren, Darla, Lynne, and Richard; And for the people who are no longer with us, Stanley, Carole, Barbara and Monte. Without you, my book would be empty pages.

Introduction

You may be familiar with the phrase, "When life gives you lemons, make lemonade." But, did you know that the concept behind that cliché is rooted in Biblical principle? Take a look at Romans 8:28.

"And we know that all things work together for good to those who love God, to those who are called according to His purpose." Romans 8:28

The verse is saying that despite our adversities, God will work to create something good. God has a way of turning lemons into lemonade. He has made a lot of lemonade in my life, for which I am eternally grateful. I hope that through reading my story you will be inspired to trust God to work for good in your life. I hope that you enjoy the sweet taste of lemonade.

Day 1

God started making my first glass of lemonade on October 22, 1969, a cool and dry Fall evening in Farmington, New Mexico. A close friend of my parents invited us to eat homemade Mexican food at her home before attending a prayer meeting that night. Our menu consisted of enchiladas, rice and beans, and I'm sure a salad too. I especially loved the sopapillas, or as I liked to call them, pillows. Not only were they delicious, but my 3-year-old imagination thought they were the perfect size on which my Barbie doll could rest her head.

Looking at his watch, my dad realized that time was moving quickly. He needed to get to the church to unlock the doors. My brother Joe, who is only 18-months older than me, asked if he could ride along with dad. The two left about an hour before mom drove my brother Lee, age 6, and me to the prayer meeting.

After eating a healthy portion of Mexican cuisine, my eyes grew heavy. Carrying me to the family's white Datsun pickup, my mom sat me on the bench seat. Seat belt laws were not mandatory or enforced, so snuggling unbuckled next to my mother, I closed my eyes. Resting his head on the passenger's side door, Lee dozed off to sleep too. As my mother drove down the windy dark road she came to a stop at the intersection at the Bloomfield Highway. "Are there any cars coming?" She asked the half-asleep Lee. All appeared safe.

Minutes later, my dad received word of a fatal automobile accident on the Bloomfield Highway. A carload of drunken teenagers were driving down the road without their headlights turned on. The darkness of the night made it impossible to see them coming. As they approached, not yielding at the intersection, they collided into our vehicle.

The report said the scene was a horrific, jumbled-up, scrap-metal nightmare. Shards of glass sprayed in all directions. The front window gaped with a shattered hole, where my body catapulted through. Two cars were squashed together like a folded up accordion. An eyewitness ran over to my mom who was pressed against the steering wheel. "Where are my children?" She gasped. Finding Lee first, and hearing my cries in the distance, the stranger ran back to tell her we were alive... Only to discover that my mother was not.

As my dad continued listening to the report, nurses were rolling me down the emergency room corridor, not expecting me to live. Losing a lot of blood caused me to lose consciousness. Time was of the essence as my frail body fought to live. Lee, shocked and scratched, but uninjured, absorbed each moment of the night.

There was no time to mourn. With three children to worry about, his youngest daughter close to death, my dad called the pastor of our church. Being a man of God, my father asked the pastor to pray over and anoint me. God sent His angels, in that desperate moment, to fight off dark forces. He wasn't finished with me yet. Within about a week, my eyes popped open, my mouth started to drool, and my stomach grumbled.

"Daddy, can I have some cottage cheese?" I asked. Those words still remain a mystery to me. Why didn't I ask for candy?! You see, my father was a dentist and had trained me well. Proverbs 22:6 says, "Train up a child in the way he should go, and when he is old he will not depart from it." Though, I'm certain if I had decided to take advantage of my fragile situation to ask for chocolate candy, he would have agreed.

A mixture of laughter and joyful tears filled the room that night. However, the doctors discovered that the injuries I sustained from being catapulted through the window would never be fully restored. My left arm was permanently paralyzed. It's hard to imagine what I can't remember: Using two hands. Sadly, I also have no memory of my birth mother.

God saved me that night and continues to orchestrate my life. Despite tragedy and physical disadvantages, I am blessed. I have gifts and abilities that I'm not even aware of yet, hidden beneath my perceived disadvantages. Because bad things happened to me, I can appreciate life more. I know that God saved me and he has a plan for my life.

It's tempting to discredit God's itinerary by hiding behind misfortune and making excuses. Have you ever caught yourself speaking or thinking the following statements?

"I'm not smart enough."

"I don't have that kind of stamina."

"I'm too ordinary."

"My health is poor."

"I'm too shy."

"I'm not old enough."

"I'm too old."

Or in my case... "I only have one hand." One of the most exciting and creative ways for me to share Jesus is to tell my story. It's a first-hand (pun intended) account of how something terrible may be used to impact others positively. October 22, 1969 happened to be a tragic night. How I choose to live despite that tragedy is the driving force of my testimony.

An old proverbial phrase that most of us are familiar with is, "When life gives you lemons make lemonade, " It's an optimistic approach for turning our adversities into our advantages. The obstacles I have encountered throughout my life are the necessary steps for me to become the person I am today. Without each experience, whether good or bad, I wouldn't have the capacity to be the real me, full of flaws and full of victory.

Time to share your lemonade:

When we share our stories with others, we allow them to see our complications and imperfect parts, and then they can feel more confident in sharing their stories. When someone takes the time to share a story, we start to see the real them.

Write a memory of a time something seemingly bad happened, yet it turned out good.

_____

_____

_____

_____

_____

_____

_____

Day 2

Lying in my bed at the San Juan Regional Hospital, in Farmington, New Mexico, bandages covering me from head to toe, a continuous "beep-beep-beep" could be heard from my heart monitor... A clear indication that I was still alive. Sleeping through the hustle and bustle of nurses coming and going to check my vital signs, while the doctors discussed hopeful options to revitalize my paralyzed arm, I continued fighting for my life. I imagine during those chaotic days in the hospital, that my fearless attitude grew in a mighty way. Though, I would still have a lot to learn.

My leaving the hospital is proof that miracles do exist. Dad continually worked hard to raise his three children as a single parent. This included driving me to routine doctor appointments as I recovered from the accident. I especially remember the day that the doctor removed my sterilized eye-bandage. A shard of glass from the accident had lodged just millimeters away from my left eye. The doctors said if the glass had dug any deeper, I would have lost my vision in that eye. I was lucky to have my vision and, at that time, we still held out hope that the use of my arm could be restored.

The medical team believed that if they could somehow stimulate the nerves in my arm, it might function again. Researching various possibilities, they introduced me to what I like to refer to as human jumper cables, or the "stimulator." The name alone sounds intimidating. The stimulator, though, was not used to restart cars, but to restart the function of my arm. Insulated cables connected my arms to a power source. On its control panel was a knob. Turning the knob to the right would strengthen the voltage. Turning it to the left would decrease the shock. The hope was that the power might "restart" my paralyzed arm.

Unawares to me, my brothers used the stimulator for other uses. During the day, they played with their G.I. Joe action figure, using the stimulator to interrogate my Barbie dolls. Knobs and switches were turned to full capacity to torture poor Barbie. She was unaffected by the currents, of course. However, my brothers forgot one important detail as they completed their game. They forgot to turn the voltage back down to the recommended frequency for my age and size.

Crawling into my bed that night, I reached for the machine and strapped it to my arm with the two attached pads. Flicking the switch on, electricity bolted at the highest possible level, causing me to scream in pain. Hearing my distress, Dad bolted into my room to discover a magnitude of electricity surging through my arm. That very moment should have been a clear indication that the stimulator would never work for me. If a shock of that value couldn't restart my arm, then we should have known right away to throw the machine out.

G.I. Joe did not get into trouble for playing with the

stimulator, but my brothers certainly did. Under no circumstances were they allowed to play with my stimulator again. Apparently God's plan for my life and the use of the stimulator were not in an agreement. Otherwise, my arm would certainly be working at this point. During the process of my healing, God was there making me strong and bold, creating my fearless attitude. That fearlessness comes from God. See what the Bible has to say about being fearless.

"Be strong and of good courage; do not fear nor be afraid of them; for the Lord your God, He is the One who goes with you. He will not leave you nor forsake you." Deuteronomy 31:6

Fear not, for I am with you; Be not dismayed, for I am your God. I will strengthen you, yes, I will help you, I will uphold you with My righteous right hand. Isaiah 41:13

The Lord is my light and my salvation; Whom shall I fear? The Lord is the strength of my life; Of whom shall I be afraid? Psalms 27:1

Time to share your lemonade:

Deuteronomy 31:6 is a great reminder that we need not fear. It also makes me laugh because it says, "Do not fear nor be afraid of *them*." In other words, I should not fear my brothers, right? The Bible also says that "vengeance is the Lords." Watch out, Lee and Joe!

What makes you feel fearless?

_____

_____

Write about a story or experience where you acted fearlessly.

_____

_____

_____

Day 3

Dad hired a nanny to take care of Lee, Joe and me while he worked. Sadly, her child caring skills were less than desirable. The woman was as nasty as an angry hornet and spoke harshly to us kids. One evening, during the boys bath routine, she grew furious with them splashing water on the floor.

"Keep the water in the tub," She said as she angrily grabbed Joe for a beating. His wiry body was too slippery, and he ran for safety.

"You are fired." Dad firmly said to the nanny. "Your actions towards my kids will not be tolerated."

The pastor's wife at our church, Mrs. Goley, heard about the situation. She knew that dad needed a loving wife, not another nanny, and she had the perfect person in mind. Barbara Gerdts, a recent widow, would be the perfect match. Soon, a plan developed to introduce the two.

In the Spring of 1968, Barbara and her husband Pastor Gene Gerdts completed an exhausting week of preaching at an evangelistic series. They had travelled several hours away from home. Being anxious to get back to their son Ty, age 8, and their comfy beds, they packed their belongings in the car and started for home. Lori, their 5-year-old daughter, cuddled with a doll in the backseat and drifted to sleep right away. Barbara could no longer fight exhaustion, and she too fell asleep. Pastor Gerdts was drained from the grueling week's event. He, too, could no longer hold his head up. The car kept moving until it impacted against a bridge, leaving Barbara a single mother.

Mrs. Goley knew both dad and Barbara had experienced similar tragedies. Being a clever matchmaker, she encouraged dad to write Barbara a letter. Sparks ignited, and letters were written. Within a month, dad proposed, and she said *yes*. On December 30, 1969, a special celebration was coordinated. Pastor and Mrs. John Goley welcomed a small group of friends to their home to witness the marriage of my father to our new mother.

Adoption papers were signed on November 10, 1970, growing the Gerdts-Rudisaile family into three boys, two girls, and two parents. My scars were still very fresh from the accident, but I found much laughter as my fearless determination and family grew.

One of my favorite early memories with my siblings took place one night when we were left home alone as our parents attended a church board meeting. They left Ty, age 11, to look after us. The house was calm, until suddenly we heard a clatter downstairs in the garage.

Ty scheduled an immediate "take action" conference with the siblings. Unanimously, we decided to find anything that could wreak havoc. Collecting our individual weapons, we trudged down the stairs in single file. We planned to use as many scare tactics as possible to appear larger in number.

Being a fearless six year-old, I grabbed the closest weapon at hand: alpine ski boots. The fighter inside me was geared and ready for war. Last in line, I followed the tribe down the stairs, around the corner, and to the dining room that leads to the garage. Hearts pounding, we eagerly waited for battle. Silence filled the room.

Ty reached for the door, and on his count we were to holler anything that came to mind. "One, two, three." Holding up his fingers, and mouthing "On your mark get set, scream."

"Ahh! Ahh! Ahhhhhhh!" Our family war cry emitted a loud eerie shrill, capable of making any foe turn and run.

Nothing happened.

The intruder was never found. Possibly it was just a mouse lurking, hunting for a tasty morsel of dog food. Or perhaps a frog hopped into a shovel. Whatever made that noise is still a mystery to this day. Yet, that night created a great camaraderie between each of us kids, and a memory that continues to bring laughter. Our fearless scrimmage may not have been welcoming to the "trespasser", but I'm certain we unwittingly entertained our guardian angels.

"Two are better than one, because they have a good reward for their labor. For if they fall, one will lift up his companion." Ecclesiastes 4:9-10a

Time to share your lemonade:

Mutual trust among friends makes for great camaraderie. God puts people in our lives for a reason. Friendships and family are some of the most important treasures we can collect.

Write about how your friends have helped you to be fearless.

_____

_____

_____

Have you ever entertained angels on a fearless "scrimmage" with friends?

_____

_____

_____

_____

Day 4

Hearing childhood stories told by other people usually sends me into a laughing fit. Especially the stories with my very first and dear friend, Kathi. Those stories are usually unpredictable by nature and full of shenanigans. We were both barely learning to walk when we first started playing together. Learning to share was the premise of our early friendship.

Kathi's grandpa, affectionately called Daddy Bob, built her a cute little rocking chair. It was the perfect size for a toddler. Rocking back and forth, Kathi let out squeals of delight and nearly flipping over every time she leaned back. Her golden locks bounced up and down while giggling. She cherished that rocker like a dog cherishes chewing on a bone.

All Kathi's happy babbling came to a sudden stop, though, the moment she saw me toddle towards her. Learning to share is a painful lesson, and suddenly life got painful for my friend. Nana, Kathi's grandma, allowed me to take a turn in Kathi's rocker. The giant monster of jealousy grew deep inside Kathi. She wasn't having it. Clutching my hair with her tiny fingers and yanking me to the floor, she regained her royal throne.

Struggling to pull myself up to a standing position, *ka-boom*, I fell down on my knees. With Kathi's little legs kicking and arms swinging, she somehow pushed me right under the rocking chair. I was pinned to the ground, imprisoned, with no way out. Kathi proceeded to rock back and forth, giggling.

A few years later, I finally received my very own white and shiny rocking chair on my fifth birthday. Just like Kathi loved her rocking chair, I also cherished mine. It's possible, if given the opportunity, I'd also kick Kathi underneath mine, too. Thankfully, that's a story that never happened.

One of the reasons my rocking chair holds so much value to me is because of the memories it brings while I was strapped to the stimulator. Those electrical currents were something I dreaded. However, during that time as I rocked in my little chair, Dad was always by my side. Each night he read me stories from my favorite set of books, *Uncle Arthur's Bedtime Stories*.

I still possess that little rocking chair. It's no longer shiny and white, yet it still remains one of my favorite gifts. Many years later, after Kathi and I grew up, I received a call from her. "I have something for you, but I can't tell you what it is yet." She said.

Through contacts of mutual friends, Kathi located the rocking chair my mom rocked me in as a newborn baby. Words cannot express the gratitude I have of this priceless gift. It more than makes up for the time she pinned me under her rocking chair.

Time to share your lemonade:

A true friend has always been one of God's most sought after gifts. Thankfully the book of Proverbs says a lot about friends. Here's just one verse.

"A man who has friends must himself be friendly, but there is a friend who sticks closer than a brother." Proverbs 18:24

I'm very proud to say Kathi and I are still friends. In fact, she's my oldest friend. (I apologize Kathi, but I just had to use "oldest" to describe you.)

Do you have a friend that means the world to you? Take a moment to share a few things that make your friend so wonderful.

_____

_____

_____

_____

Day 5

Canyonlands National Park in Moab, Utah, is arguably the most magical, yet most peculiar, place in the Southwestern United States. It has rivers, arches, petroglyphs, and mesas... The perfect setting for my parents to discover I was fearless. Every Fall, a group from our church planned annual camping trips to this enchanted location.

My childhood hiking skills were daring. Nothing intimidated me. Running and leaping from the edges of cliffs with steep-drop offs put a whole new reverence for God in my mom. She worshipped Him in a most terrifying way during our camping trips. Gritting her teeth, heart pounding, and knees knocking, every time I climbed she prayed, "Oh Lord, keep her safe."

Each day started with a campfire, pancakes and hot chocolate. Then, loading into the *Jeeps*, we drove for about an hour to a massive rock formation with a huge hole in it. This formation is known as "Paul Bunyan's Potty." Dad reminded me not to climb straight up, or my climbing would lead to disaster. He reminded me to climb at a gradual angle. I nodded, eyes wide with excitement.

Scrambling out of the cars, our mass of energetic hikers trudged down an old washed-out road that led to large cliffs. Thick vegetation guarded the cliff against intruders, but we soon discovered an opening. With each step, we ascended closer to our destination: The arch with a massive hole resembling a toilet. It was approximately 150 to 200 feet from the ground. Finding a shaded area to stop for a drink of water, we surveyed the scenery. Native American ruins nestled right ahead.

A steep incline led the way up to the ruins. Hiking the last stretch definitely wasn't for the weak of heart. The best way to climb was to gradually scale the area back and forth; Slow and steady; One foot at a time.

My mother chose not to climb. She stayed below on a flat surface. Looking up, she noticed a tiny figure climbing straight up the incline, not going back and forth as instructed. She immediately recognized it as me and gasped, "Lord, save that child."

Fingers clawing at anything I could grasp, I suddenly began my unplanned dissension. Tiny pebbles and sand flung in the air. Slipping faster to the edge of the cliff, I tried to find something to grip hold of, but there was nothing. The traction on my shoes could not stop me, causing my pants to fray and leaving a pink abrasion on my legs.

My friend Ken immediately saw my demise and took action. Climbing the last stretch the correct way, gradually from side to side, he planted his feet firmly as I skidded closer to him. Reaching out his hand, and grabbing a hold of my foot, he helped me to slow down and halt to a stop. From that day forward Ken was my hero.

All's well that ends well, however, there were consequences to not following instructions. My legs were significantly scraped and my pants ruined as a reminder for me to listen to my parents. If we don't follow rules there can be a lot of chaos.

"Children, obey your parents in the Lord, for this is right." Ephesians 6:1

Time to share your lemonade:

We all have choices, but with those choices come consequences. That's why our parents, as well as our Heavenly Father, sets out rules for us to follow. They help us live a better life.

Write about something bad that happened when you ignored the rules.

_____

_____

_____

_____

Day 6

Storytelling is my brother Lee's God-given talent. However, there is at least one story he has completely misconstrued over the years. Being able to stretch the truth and make it believable is a real skill for him. He laughs and attests that his version of the modernized "Lady Godiva story" is true. I laugh too, but I question some of the details. My brother and I will have to agree to disagree on this memory.

The legend goes that in the Thirteenth Century, a noblewoman named Lady Godiva rode her horse along the streets covered with nothing but her long hair. The citizens under her husband's government were oppressed with a huge taxation. Lady Godiva appealed over and over to her husband to lift the taxes. He finally agreed to her request, but only if she rode the streets with only her hair covering her.

Fast forward to the Twentieth Century, when I was a 5-year-old with short hair, Lee and Joe dared me to run around the yard without my shirt after seeing the neighbor boys playing in the adjacent pasture.

"We dare you to run around the backyard without your shirt." They badgered me. We lived in the country. In the far distance the neighbor boys were so far away that they appeared only inches tall. Therefore, I accepted the challenge. Here's the part of Lee's story that's shady. In his own words, "Joe ran to the shed and revved up the riding lawn mower. The engine was bellowing loudly, as he yelled, 'hop on Mary!' Climbing on the hood of the tractor, she rode topless as he chauffeured her around the property line."

Lee still laughs hysterically that I accepted the challenge. However, his memory won't hold up in the court of law. Joe is only 18 months older than me. Me riding a tractor driven by toddler Joe would have been like me riding a mechanical bull. I wouldn't have remained for very long. The possibility of lawn chairs, plants, toys, and myself all turning to mulch would have been incredibly high.

My brother's "Lady Godiva" narrative has no validity. Here's the truth, I accepted the dare. I took my top off, ran several yards out in the yard, and then back to the porch to cover up. The incident took less than a minute. Yes, Lee's story is funnier than mine. I love listening to him laugh while telling the fable of me riding on a mower. He loves to convince his listeners that his story is the truth. Regardless of whose story is true, my "Lady Godiva" experience has an underlying message of being pressured into something seemingly harmless. We all have been tempted to do things we know are wrong. For me running outside with my shirt off may not seem to be an obvious wrong for a five-year-old, but if it were the right thing to do, I wouldn't need to be dared.

Matthew 26:41 says "Watch and pray, lest you enter into temptation. The spirit indeed is willing, but the flesh is weak."

Time to share your lemonade:

We have all been tempted to break the rules from time to time. It's important to remember that rules are made for a reason, even if breaking the rules seems like it may be harmless. For example, although I was very young, it was still important for me to be respectful of my body in this story. True enough, I didn't get in trouble and no one got hurt, but I was still learning the concept of respecting my own and other people's bodies. It may not always be a teasing brother at an innocently young age asking you to do something uncomfortable. If anyone ever makes you feel uncomfortable by asking you to do something you don't want to do, take courage in knowing that it's ok to say no and walk away. If you still feel weird afterwards, or if you don't feel safe, always ask for help from an adult.

Can you think of a time when you were peer-pressured into something? How did you respond?

_____

_____

Is it easier to stand up to friends or to strangers when you disagree? Why?

_____

_____

If you feel like something is wrong, is it ok to do it anyway if a friend or even an adult tries to make you do it? _____

_____

_____

What advice would you give to someone dealing with negative peer pressure?

_____

_____

Day 7

During the summers I played outside a lot. My favorite activities included playing in the irrigation ditch, building forts out of bales of hay, playing baseball with my siblings, and hanging out with my neighbor Kathi in her grandpa's pasture. Between playing in the dirt and being out in the sun, my skin became very dirty, or so I thought.

My sister, Lori, also played outside, but she had very fair skin while mine got dark in the sun. Noticing there was a difference between my skin and Lori's skin, I asked her, "How do you stay so clean?"

In great detail, Lori explained her hygiene regime very seriously, step by step. "Soak in the bathtub for at least 30 minutes. Make sure you have soap and a coarse washcloth; also scrub the layers of dead skin." Teaching me how to properly bathe made Lori feel important. She too desired to see me clean after I ran around all day in the dirt and grass.

"You might have to take two hot baths in a row for you to get as clean as me. You are pretty dirty. Keep scrubbing though. Don't give up. Every night, soak and scrub." My sister encouraged me to get clean. Perhaps she was embarrassed of all that dirt, I don't know. However, she was very kind and made sure I followed her instructions. Thinking I should grab two washcloths, I ran to the linen closet. I thought, "Two will be good just in case the first one gets really gross and muddy."

I soaked, scrubbed, and repeated every single day for a week. Still, my skin color did not change. I didn't yet realize that the difference in our appearances wasn't a matter of dirt, but that we were simply created differently. Discouraged about my unchanged condition, I remembered a Bible story my parents read to me from 2 Kings chapter 5.

It's the story of when Naaman, the commander of the Syrian army, contracted leprosy. Prophet Elisha told him to go dip in the Jordan River seven times. Resisting at first, he changed his mind and finally bathed in the Jordan. After seven complete dips he was healed. I thought to myself, "I'm going to be like Naaman, and dip in the bathtub seven times. If he can be cured from his skin condition, then I can be cured of mine."

Taking a big breath of air, I submerged under a sea of bubbles. Tidal waves of water splashing out of the tub as I plunged seven times. Just like Naaman, I checked for observable signs of improvements. Seven times I dropped underwater, seven times my condition remained the same.

After scrubbing, dunking, and practically drowning, my skin was definitely cleaner than Lori's skin. I had failed to remember that we were created differently. God made us to be unique masterpieces. My "dirty skin" was clean, I just hadn't discovered that we are all created to be unique.

Time to share your lemonade:

Not only are we all created to be unique, but we are also all created to be equal. We need to celebrate the things that make us different, rather than dwell on them as negative things. See what the Bible has to say about it.

"I will praise You, for I am fearfully and wonderfully made; Marvelous are Your works, And that my soul knows very well." Psalm 139:14

I love that we are all fearfully and wonderfully made. Remember to treat others as you would be treated, celebrating the many different cultures and people of the world. God created us all to be unique and marvelous. Remember to show kindness, always. Remember that you are loved, exactly how you are.

What does it mean to celebrate the things that make us different?

_____

_____

_____

Day 8

Long prayers and children go together like orange juice flavored toothpaste. I bet your nose is turning up right now. My nose turned up as a six-year-old girl kneeling through long church prayers. While trying to be reverent, I grew weary and impatient as my knees developed carpet burns from all my wiggling.

My vocabulary didn't have the word "gossip" written in it yet, but kneeling during those long prayers at my family's church taught me the concept. Names and deeds were mentioned one right after the other in what seemed to me a less-than-prayerful manner to me. *Amens* echoed in the sanctuary, and I still struggled to keep my eyes closed. I don't know how my dad knew, maybe it was that tiny angel standing on his right shoulder whispering, "*Pssst* Mary has her eyes open," but immediately dad tapped me on the shoulder. "Close your eyes, Mary Ellen."

The next day, while playing with my friend Kathi, I mentioned, "I really don't like the long prayers at church."

Kathi, 45-days older than me and with much more maturity, provided me with her thought provoking insight. "Do what I do," she suggested. "Shout out 'Amen' when you want the prayer to end. People do it all the time."

The following week, sitting in separate pews, we gave each other the nod to affirm that our plan was set in motion.

"Open your Bibles to "Ecclesiastes 4:9," The Deacon said and began reading, "Two are better than one because they have a good reward for their labor."

What luck? I couldn't believe my ears. Kathi and I were two people so our *amens* could be rewarded. "No long prayer today," I hoped. As soon as the deacon opened his mouth to pray, "Dear…" We began shouting, "Amen!"

Without fear or trembling, the two of us echoed *amen* one right after the other. Our *amens* grew stronger and louder. Keeping my eyes shut tight, I still felt the glare of disapproval from my dad. I didn't care though. I had scripture on my side.

"Oh Lord in Heaven, we come to you asking for your healing over brother Dan…"

"Amen!" I said.

On the other side of the church, I heard Kathi's voice echoing out her "Amen."

"We also lift up Edith and Luis during their time of financial need…" Our "Amens" got a little louder.

"Baby Emily was taken from her family last week."

"Amen," I shouted. My dad reached over and thumped me real hard on the head. Then, not only did my knees hurt, but my head was throbbing, too. Neither Kathi nor I had a clue of the whole concept of what *amen* means. That thump on the head was followed up with a stern swat on my behind after prayer. That was the last day I tried to end prayer early.

Time to share your lemonade:

It is important to pray for others and their needs, just as it is important to show respect during prayer. What I didn't realize in those long prayers was that my yelling was just as bad, if not worse, than what I believed to be gossip in the prayer requests. In fact, God wants us to pray for our friends and loved ones. Rather than mindlessly repeating the same prayers, lovingly consider the needs of others and pray for all those around you.

Therefore I encourage first of all that supplications, prayers, intercessions, and giving of thanks be made for all people. 1 Timothy 2:1

Take a moment to write a list of people you would like to remember in your prayers.

_____

_____

_____

_____

Day 9

One of the most endearing qualities of my dad was his passion to help people who couldn't afford dental work. He routinely flew his airplane to a Navajo Reservation at Crownpoint, New Mexico, where he volunteered his time at LaVida Mission, a boarding school for Navajo children. On many occasions, people would trade their goods for his dental services.

After flying into the Mission, and working on a couple of patient's teeth, a man approached dad with a 3-foot tall Shetland pony, the color of a saltine cracker.

"Dr. Rudisaile, I have no money, but I will give you Crackers, my little pony for payment."

Accepting the offer, my dad replied, "That sounds like a fair bargain. I have five children who will love this little pony."

I'm not sure how the pony made it home, but living in the country made our home the ideal place to welcome Crackers. Our property included a little cement pond on five acres, granting easy access for the little pony to drink and eat at leisure.

Brushing and feeding were daily chores for my siblings. Dad thought I was too young to take care of Crackers on my own. I was just five-years old. He gave me explicit instructions not to play with him alone. "Crackers is a small pony, but very strong. If you're not careful, he will hurt you," dad warned.

One evening, as my parents were leaving to attend a church meeting, they left instructions on how to contact them in case of an emergency. Before cell phones, most homes had landlines. Phones were attached to walls without caller ID or contacts. The numbers were published once a year in a book called, "The Southwestern Bell Telephone Book." Emergency phone numbers were handwritten on the back of our book for easy access.

After my dad and mom left, I slipped out the back door to play with Crackers, all by myself. Sneaking up behind him without warning, was not one of my most brilliant ideas.

The pony let out a startled, "Neigh!" He reared up on his hind legs and struck me to the ground, leaving a hoof mark on my back. Excruciating pain shot right through me. Blood dripped all over my favorite shirt. "Oh no, What will dad say?" I thought.

Hearing the commotion outside, Ty and Lee ran to rescue me from the frightened pony. Carrying me into the house, to stop the bleeding. Picking up the phone receiver, Ty dialed the number to the church.

"Dad, something happened…"

I quickly learned why playing with Crackers alone wasn't a smart idea. A hoof print scar on my back and a ruined shirt were obvious implications of what a Shetland pony can do to a small child, such as myself.

Time to share your lemonade:

All through life, we humans tend to learn lessons the hard way. My dad knew that playing with Crackers alone was not a good idea, yet I didn't listen to his warning. In the future, I was more careful. Think of the pain that could have been saved, though, if I had just been obedient in the first place!

"Obey those who rule over you, and be submissive, for they watch out for your souls, as those who must give account. Let them do so with joy and not with grief, for that would be unprofitable for you." Hebrews 13:17

Write about a time when you learned something the hard way, through trial and error.

_____

_____

_____

_____

Day 10

Being a daddy's girl, I always felt safe and secure when my dad was around. No one made me feel as protected as my father... Except during the night. I was very afraid of the dark. I didn't even like sleeping with Teddy Bears because I feared they might turn into "monsters" after dark.

Before first grade, night time was particularly worrisome. My curtains had to be fully closed, closet door shut, nothing on the floor, and most importantly, my bedroom door left open. However, there was one night that I decided to sleep with my Teddy.

"Daddy, will you get Teddy for me?" I asked as my dad said good night. Tucking me into bed, dad prayed with me and gave me a kiss on the forehead. "Sleep tight, don't let the bed bugs bite." He said. Drifting off to sleep and hugging my bear tight, I began to dream. Kicking and twisting, my covers ended up falling on the floor. My cold feet woke me up. Patting around my bed, I felt for my sheets and blanket. Noticing a brown unidentified object in my bed, I screeched, "Daddy, help!"

I didn't need to keep yelling. He sensed the urgency in my voice, and came running. When I saw his shadow in the doorway, I blurted out, "There's cow manure in my bed!"

A quick switch of the light showed that the manure was actually my fluffy Teddy Bear.

I don't remember my dad laughing or getting mad that I woke him up. I do know that he heard my cry, came to my room, and turned on the light to show that I was safe from any danger.

"Cows will not open a locked door, climb up the stairs to your bedroom, and leave manure in a bed without my knowledge." He assured.

Just like my dad that night, our Heavenly Father hears our cries for help. He meets us where we are and sheds light on all of our fears. Nothing takes place without His knowledge, and we can take courage in his love.

"He restores my soul; He leads me in the paths of righteousness for His name's sake. Yea, though I walk through the valley of the shadow of death, I will fear no evil; for You are with me; Your rod and Your staff, they comfort me" Psalms 23:3-4

Time to share your lemonade:

Sleeping with cow manure is pretty silly. I'd like to think I'm not the only one who experiences crazy stories, or the only one that's ever been afraid.

Write about a time when you felt afraid, and about how you overcame that fear.

Day 11

Some of the most unsuspecting people have "legendary" stories to share. My siblings claim mine is more of an "infamous" account. They like it when I appear as a hardened criminal. This notorious tale happened before I joined the ranks of education with my siblings.

Periodically, my mom helped dad in his dental office. During those occasions, I stayed at home with the cleaning lady, Mrs. Rowe. While she was busy cleaning, my imagination grew into a creative ticking-time-bomb, ready to explode at any minute. Being alone in our big house, my creativity and curiosity took flight. I went sliding down the stairs as if I were riding a waterfall. I covered the sides of my canopy bed to pretend I was in a cold damp cave. I climbed bookshelves as if they were mountains. Dissociating myself from the reality of being home without my siblings allowed me to explore and investigate possibilities of the unknown.

One of those adventurous days, when I was climbing a "mountain", a box of matches, caught my eye. "Whoa, this will be fun!" I thought. Grabbing the box, I quickly ran to my bedroom and quietly shut the door behind me. Remembering each step my dad used to start campfires, I made a mental checklist. Kindling gathered: Check. Firewood stacked: Check. Fire starter poured: Check. And finally matches: Check. I was ready to start my very own fire.

My pink plastic trash made the best pretend fire pit. Waded papers and tissues took the place of kindling and firewood, and my perfume from Nana Wilkes assisted with starting my fire. One strike of a match and my fire would be ablaze, I imagined.

Picking up a match, and striking it across the rough edge of the box, a bright orange flame flared up and then died. Striking matches while watching the flames die over and over gave me an adrenaline rush. "I'll try lighting a match one more time." I decided.

My 6-year-old life got very interesting as soon as the match hit the matchbox. The flame ignited. Dropping the lit match right on top of all waded paper and kleenexes caused smoke to billow. I did not consider my "imaginary" kindling and firewood would burn so easily. The pretty pink trash can was a big flaming ball of melting plastic.

Frantically dancing up and down with fire in hand, blowing on the flames, I put my trash can down on my bed to open the window. Instantly my bed caught on fire. The Holly Hobby Doll bedspread had a hole burned right through it. Suddenly I wasn't having fun. Reality got really scary fast.

Below my window, Mrs. Rowe had stepped out to sweep the front porch. She looked up just in time to see a glowing "pink fire pit" soar past her head. Shifting her eyes to my bedroom window, she saw a silhouette of a scared child fighting another fire.

Quick on her feet, she ran up the stairs to my room and smothered the fire with her broom. The only significant damage was my trash can and my bedspread. There's no doubt God was protecting our home that particular day.

I received a spanking for that incident. Right before the hand hit my "bum" I heard my dad say, "This is going to hurt me more than it will hurt you." It's hard for children to understand that concept. "The punishment is out of love? Yeah right!"

As Christians, when we do things that aren't in our best interest, we sometimes question God's discipline to our actions. He responds, "I love you and I don't want you to keep doing this thing you're doing." The spanking I received that day served as a reminder for me not to play with matches.

"Now no chastening seems to be joyful for the present, but painful; nevertheless, afterward it yields the peaceable fruit of righteousness to those who have been trained by it." Hebrews 12:11

Time to share your lemonade:

Share a disciplinary action you received and what lesson you learned from it.

_____

_____

_____

_____

_____

_____

_____

_____

_____

Day 12

My father planned many camping adventures. We packed the *Winnebago*, our camper, with all the necessary supplies to drive into the country. Once when we were gone on one of our excursions, we had an unexpected house sitter.

Sunday evening we pulled up to our house about seven or eight o'clock. During clean-up instructions, Dad noticed something wasn't right. The back, French, glass door to our home was shattered. "Someone broke into our home," he announced.

Dad cautiously stepped out to take a closer look. Every step he took, five little munchkins followed. Walking straight up to the broken door, he kept marching while searching for the culprit. Feeling protected in his shadow, each one of us kids marched close behind him. As long as he was leading we were following.

"Watch out for all the glass," he warned us.

Carefully stepping around broken pieces of glass, we walked through the kitchen. We noticed a trail of dark round pellets leading into the library. Evidence of chewed apples scattered on the floor. Someone had been hungry.

By this time, the story of "The Three Little Bears" was dancing in my imagination. "Did Goldilocks break into our home? Had she found the perfect porridge? chair? and bed? I crossed my fingers that my bed was untouched as we explored the destruction of our home.

The five of us kids, still following dad, heard munching sounds from the library. Our intruder was enjoying a crunchy snack in there at that very moment. What could an intruder possibly be eating in the library? A book? Furniture? Homework?

Dad quietly pushed open the door, and we all tiptoed in a single file to see what might be around the corner. What did our curious eyes behold? One Billy goat, standing right in the middle of a floor covered with books and goat droppings. Books were knocked off of shelves, and pages were ripped into confetti. Mr. Billy Goat was very startled at our staring. His expression said it all, "You can't prove I did this, I'm innocent."

Dad always encouraged us to feed our mind with books. Mr. Billy Goat took that phrase a little too literally. "No, Billy! Don't eat books! READ them!"

God knows that we will face many challenges, tests, and trials. He knew that we'd experience moments of uncertainty; for example, walking into a broken into home. Like my dad leading his family through the broken glass, God will lead us through our mess.

"I will say of the Lord, 'He is my refuge and my fortress; My God, in Him I will trust.'" Psalm 91:2

Time to Share your lemonade:

How have you sensed God leading you?

Day 13

Keeping a good babysitter was a challenge for my parents. To say I'm innocent of any mischievousness is to bear false witness. Out of all five of us kids, Lori was the most innocent. The rest of us exhibited what I like to call "irreverent behavior." We lacked properness and seriousness.

My three brothers were ornery characters that seemed larger than life. Their reputation preceded them, making babysitters few and hard to come by. Those boys once tied a lady who was taking care of us to a large tree in the middle of our pasture. We lived out in the country, no amount of yelling could save her. Eventually, Mom and Dad drove down our long private lane and noticed the victim bound to the tree. No amount of payment lured potential babysitters to agree to take care of us, except for Vergie James. Elderly and frail, Vergie agreed to care for us. My six-year-old eyes thought she was 90 years old, but in reality, I'm sure she was closer to age 70.

My parents had built a large two-story home to accommodate all their kids. One of our favorite pastimes when the parents were away was sliding down the stairs. We found boxes, cookie sheet trays, garbage bags… You name it, we tried it. Sliding down the stairs became a rowdy sport. A high stakes competition.

One day, Vergie James decided to join us in our forbidden extracurricular activity. She was a brave old soul, as she grabbed hold of the cardboard box and yelled "yippee" all the way to the bottom. She was a gem. As long as she joined in our game of sliding, we couldn't get in trouble.

Vergie also liked taking us for a drive for soft serve ice cream. She drove a small compact car from the late 1960s, probably something like a Ford Falcon. There was no air conditioner, but if we rolled all the windows down then we enjoyed 60 mph winds. Believe me, this little old lady knew how to put the pedal to the metal.

Before leaving our driveway, Vergie always said, "Y'all roll down your glasses."

The only one who wore eyeglasses at the time was Joe. He put his hand up to the side of his glasses making the circular motion as if he were trying to roll down his glasses. "They're not rolling down Vergie." He said.

"That's funny, they worked just the other day," She replied.

"Look Vergie! Suki is sitting on top of your car." One of us yelled. I don't remember who spotted our German Shepard first, but right in the middle of her hood was our dog, Suki. He climbed up and sat there looking at us looking at him. Refusing to get off her car, Vergie hammered her foot on the gas pedal. The G-force pushed all of us back into the seat and instantly lunged forward when she slammed on the brakes. Suki rolled off the car confused, but trotted off to the yard unharmed.

Vergie James was a legendary babysitter. She can be compared to no other... AKA best babysitter ever. The tiny elderly lady had more spunk than any of our teenage babysitters. She knew that it was ok to have fun and to be a little silly, especially when babysitting a handful of unruly children. Vergie James was a legendary babysitter indeed, mostly because of her happy spirit.

"A merry heart does good, like medicine, But a broken spirit dries the bones." Proverbs 17:22

Time to share your lemonade:

Write a memory of someone in your life who has a merry heart. What makes them legendary in your eyes?

_____

_____

_____

Day 14

Canyonlands National Park in Utah is the setting for many of my fondest memories. It was the place where friends and family looked forward to camping and exploring together. Camper trailers, tents, and four-wheel drives were all packed and ready for a weekend's voyage. Adventure awaited for all who set out to go camping.

Known for its dramatic scenic landscapes, Canyonlands is a perfect spot for the hiking enthusiast. Large flat mesas stretch as far as the eye can see. Buttes carved out of the Colorado River, and primitive enchanted deserts create a beautiful destination getaway from daily routine.

On one of our Canyonlands camping excursions, a caravan of four-wheel drives lined up on the dusty roads, ready to head out to Bryce Canyon. Among the motorcade was our brand new 1972 GMC Blazer. The dusty road we traveled on transcended into a narrow slanted rocky terrain.

Advancing further on the rugged trails made our four-wheeling extra scary. Any wrong move and our Blazer would slide off the beaten track, and possibly flip over. Bodies bouncing, mom clinching the dashboard, and breaths held, dad steadily drove our Blazer into the dangerous unknown. As the trail narrowed, a drop-off on the passengers' side appeared.

Sliding to the edge of the trail, dad kept trudging. Veering closer to the drop-off, my mom no longer held her breath. She yelled, "Watch out!" Staying focused on the road, dad never flinched. He delivered us through the roughest spot unharmed.

Back at the campsites that night, near mishaps were the main subject around our campfire. Marshmallows roasted over hot flames as songs erupted. Then a snake quietly slithered through our tents. Several yards away in the dark, a scream of terror pierced the air.

"Snake!"

Screams echoed in the canyon as campers leaped for safety. Grabbing a shovel, dad severed the head from the snake's body. He knew the heads of venomous snakes can still bite several hours after decapitation. As a precaution, dad dug a hole and buried the entire snake.

In the early morning, we discovered the snake body had wiggled itself free from its burial site. Seeing the snake's body in postmortem movement, gave me goosebumps. Can you imagine what would happen if the fangs were the part moving around? My story might have ended entirely differently. It's clear that God takes care of his children. Canyonlands memories are evidence of His protection.

"Behold, I am with you and will keep you wherever you go, and will bring you back to this land; for I will not leave you until I have done what I have spoken to you."
Genesis 28:15

Time to share your lemonade:

Tell of an intense moment where things could have gone wrong, but, with God's help, everything turned out ok.

Day 15

Sunday, April 4th, 1973, we kids awoke to no pancakes. Every Sunday morning, as a breakfast tradition, mom usually made pancakes. However, today was different. The kitchen was empty. Where was our mother? Why was there no breakfast? We were hungry and wanted to eat.

As we sat at an empty table, dad came into the kitchen. Five sets of eyes stared blankly in his direction. "Your baby brother Daren Gregory was born early this morning," He announced. Instantly forgetting about our growling tummies, we cheered.

"When can we meet him?"

The hospital rules stated, "No children under 12 years old allowed." Those rules didn't stop us from seeing Daren, though. Outside mom's hospital window was a tree the boys were able to climb, while dad lifted Lori and me on his shoulders. Wrapped tightly in a blue hospital blanket, Mom held Daren to the window. Straightaway, he had 5 sibling-bodyguards ready to protect him. On that day we decreed him "Daren Gregory the golden child."

After Daren started walking, and gaining independence, he toddled off without being noticed. Everyone kept busy with chores, homework or music lessons as he disappeared. Thirty minutes to an hour slipped away before someone realized he was missing.

"Hey, where's Daren?" Joe asked.

Adrenaline pumped through our veins as we all rushed to find our baby brother. Each one of us called out his name, "Daren!" Searching the irrigation ditch, back yard, pasture, and all the rooms in the house lead us to nothing. We prayed as we combed every inch of the property. Just as mom frantically picked up the phone to call for help, someone yelled, "I found him!"

Hiding between the wall and couch in the living room, our baby brother slept. Typically the living room was reserved for only special events. Daren must have thought a nap warranted as a special occasion. Needing a quiet place away from all the hustle and bustle of his older siblings, he found the perfect spot. That afternoon, our emotions were rampant while scouting for Daren. We all were scared of his unknown demise, and then later relieved when he was found safe and sound behind the couch. We were all his protectors, a responsibility we have taken seriously throughout his life.

Just like my siblings and I took responsibility for Daren very seriously, God takes protecting us even more seriously. That's why He sends His angels to watch over us. I certainly thought of myself as a guardian of Daren, although my siblings and I are not angels by any means. Unlike my siblings and I, God knew where my lost baby brother was the entire time he was missing. We can feel safe because He knows where we are at all times and is looking out for our well-being.

"For it is written: 'He shall give His angels charge over you to keep you, and, 'In their hands they shall bear you up, lest you dash your foot against a stone.'" Luke 4:10.

Time to share your lemonade:

Can you think of a time when God sent someone to help you? Perhaps you were separated from your family, or maybe you lost a pet. Write about your story.

_____

_____

_____

_____

_____

_____

_____

Day 16

Pre-adolescent years can be an awkward and clumsy time for a child. For example, bruises on my legs were evidence of me having bumped into objects. Scabs on my knees continued the tale of my clumsiness. First impressions more than likely made people think I was overly active, and a very clumsy, child.

The truth is that I was looking for adventure. Navajo Lake is a location where many of my early adventures took place. The lake had a lot to offer, such as camping, boating, fishing, hiking, and of course, me falling on cactus.

In New Mexico, there are a wide variety of cacti. The prickly pear is one of the most common cacti. I still vividly remember all the times when a sharp needle pierced through my skin. Tears often ran down my cheeks from the piercing pain.

My family spent many weekends at Navajo Lake. Each visit, my dad cautioned me to be careful, "Slow down and watch your step." No matter how hard I tried to remain upright, I alway slid and landed flat on the ground, directly on top of sharp needles.

I remember specifically thinking, "This time I'm not going to fall." and without fail, I ALWAYS tripped and landed on a cactus. My gravitational attraction to cactus was painful. While hiking, minding my own business, gravity always pulled me down. Falling happened so many times that my family started poking fun of me.

"Hey Mary, look, one of your landing pads." They joked pointing to a prickly pear.

Honestly, I did my best to avoid cacti, because removing the spears wedged in my derrière, otherwise known as my rear end, hurt more than anything. Not only was the removal painful, but it was also embarrassing when dad pulled them out.

Falling on cactus reminds me of how easy it is to fall into temptation. If we aren't looking or paying attention, it's too easy to be impulsive, and make unwise decisions. The only way to protect ourselves is to put on the armor of God. We can do that by developing a relationship with Him. Our relationship with God grows when we read the Bible, pray daily, and serve Him in all we do. My challenge to you is to put on the full armor of God: truth, righteousness, peace, faith, salvation, and the Spirit of God. While wearing a full suit of armor, cactus needles are a lot less of a threat.

"Put on the whole armor of God, that you may be able to stand against the wiles of the devil." Ephesians 6:11

Time to share your lemonade:

As a child, I always fell into cactus plants. What kind of trouble do you often find yourself falling into?

_____

_____

_____

_____

Write a list of ways that you can put on the armor of God. (For example, by being nice to a friend, or by telling the truth.)

_____

_____

_____

_____

Day 17

The Bible talks about the many ways we can praise God. For example, shouts of joy, clapping of hands, singing, and playing musical instruments, are just a few ways we can honor God. My dad chose to make sure his kids learned how to praise the Lord, by providing us with mandatory music lessons. Before making the music lessons announcement to us, my dad read from scripture.

"Praise Him with the sound of the trumpet; Praise Him with the lute and harp! Praise Him with the timbrel and dance; Praise Him with stringed instruments and flutes! Praise Him with loud cymbals; Praise Him with clashing cymbals! Let everything that has breath praise the Lord. Praise the Lord!" Psalms 150:3-6

Imagine all the clatter five kids made as we individually praised the Lord with trumpet, trombone, baritone, saxophone, and flute, each playing different songs at the same time. Every afternoon, our opposing instruments clashed against each other as we practiced in separate rooms. Only a loving God would enjoy a mixture of such squawking sounds.

Mr. Plum, an elderly short and stout gentleman, was our first music instructor. He listened to our pitchy-novice music with pride. His encouraging enthusiasm reminded us to, "Practice, practice, practice." This also became our mom and dad's mantra.

Before Mr. Plum saw my family to its fullest musical potential, he moved away. My parents started to look for our next music teacher. Teaching such a large and mischievous group of siblings was a daunting task, especially since my parents needed a teacher who would be able to come to our house for lessons. Thankfully, they found someone who was up to the task, Mr. Mitzelfelt. His musical background was very impressive and even surpassed mom and dad's expectations.

Oftentimes, Mr. Mitzelfelt brought his young son, Monte to our lessons. My tolerance for younger kids reached its limit with that boy. Being a mature three years older gave me the right to be annoyed with his non-stop activity. Watching him dart in and out of our rooms, and running up and down the stairs, one might think our house was a playground.

My patience came to its limit the moment I saw him race in and out of the bathroom, forgetting to flush the toilet. I remember telling a friend, "I'm so glad he's not my brother." My words weren't honoring or praising the Lord, but that was a lesson I was still learning.

The opposite of praise is forgetting. That means forgetting to be kind, honoring, building-up, and worshiping. I found fault in Monte and forgot to be kind. Even though he didn't hear me, my choice of words were the opposite of praise. The purpose of our music lessons was to learn a new way of expressing praise, I did the opposite.

Living a life of praise is not only the most enjoyable way to live, but it's also the most powerful way to change your life. When you're praising God, you're remembering the things He has done, you're acknowledging who He is. As you continue to praise and worship Him, things like fear and anxiety fade away.

"Make a joyful shout to the Lord, all you lands! Serve the Lord with gladness; Come before His presence with singing." Psalms 100:1-2

Time to share your lemonade:

Has there been a time you forgot to praise and instead did something opposite of praise? If you could, what would you do differently?

_____

_____

_____

Day 18

When I was in elementary school, my mornings generally started with free dance lessons. Don't be jealous, my dance instructors were my brothers Lee and Joe. They had no formal dance training, nor could they dance. However, they decided they wanted to give me a lesson.

While waiting at the bus stop, they threw tiny pebbles at my feet. I had two choices, to voluntarily dance, aka dodge the tiny rocks, or suffer through the gravel pelting at my feet. I chose to dance. My dancing performance was well-received by the early morning traffic. Many of those drivers honked showing support for my dancing education. My brothers thought it was hilarious watching me twirl around on the side of the road.

One specific morning in October, while I was hopping up and down dodging those tiny rocks, my dad drove by our bus stop. He was on his way to the airport to fly his airplane. With a toothbrush in his mouth, he waved as he drove by. My dance lessons were interrupted by waving arms and us kids shouting, "Good-bye dad!" Everyone was excited to see him. I was the only one that did not show it.

A combination of waking up on the wrong side of the bed and not wanting to be teased by my brothers made me sulky. Throughout the day, I remember wishing I would have started my day in a better mood. I was disappointed with myself for not saying goodbye to dad. Seeing my father in the evening, gave me something to look forward to at the end of my grumpy day. I couldn't wait to give him a big hug. The countdown started five, four, three, two, finally only one more hour until I would see dad. Time kept moving though, and my dad didn't come home.

Noticing it was past the time that my dad usually arrived home from work, I asked, while eating supper with my family, "Where's daddy?"

Suddenly, the phone rang, as if it were eavesdropping on my question. The image of mom answering the call left an unforgettable imprint on my mind. "Hello," A long silence filled the air as her face grew grim. Her rosy complexion turned ghostly white while she gasped out, "No!"

Hanging up the phone and repeating the report to us, mom cried, "Dad was in a plane crash, and his prognosis is not good." We all felt sick to our stomachs.

Excusing myself from the table, I ran into the living room and threw myself on the floor. "Jesus, Please save my dad!" I believed that a full recovery would take place. My childlike faith did not waver.

Mom drove three hours to the trauma hospital in Albuquerque to be with dad. Believing we'd hear good news from her later that night, the rest of us stayed home to pray for a miracle. There was no doubt in my mind that my dad would return home. I needed to hug him and tell him, "I'm sorry for not waving to you this morning." Also, I needed my dad because I had already lost my mother in a tragic accident. Losing both parents was out of the question.

Early the next morning while still in bed, I heard Lori crying loudly from her room. It was at that unpredicted moment I knew my dad wasn't ever coming back home. My heart shattered into a million pieces. I wanted to know why my prayers hadn't been answered. I couldn't even ask my dad, "Why did this happen?"

In the midst of heartache and pain, we all had to face a future without our dad. None of us understood why God allowed this horrible thing to happen. In some unknown way, God determined it was his time. I don't like it, but I have to believe that God knows what He's doing. The goodness of God is all around us. It only comes into question when bad things happen. I'm looking forward to a beautiful reunion with my dad when I can dance right into his arms and say, "I love you, daddy."

Deuteronomy 29:29 "The secret things belong to the Lord our God, but those things which are revealed belong to us and to our children forever...."

Time to share your lemonade:

Write a list of God's goodness in your life so when bad things happen you will have a reminder of something positive.

_____

_____

_____

_____

_____

_____

_____

_____

Day 19

"Dark-thirty" is a term I use to describe an unknown time of the night. For example: While sleeping peacefully in your comfy bed, you might hear a loud noise. If you don't know what time it is, and you're too afraid to open your eyes to check, then you could just say that it's "dark-thirty." I may have a fearless attitude, but there's something about "dark-thirty" that scares me. Even as an adult, I sometimes find myself running to my car when I have to leave my house before the sun comes up. Locking the doors and turning up the radio somehow makes me feel safe.

As a small child, my distaste for "dark-thirty" began when my mom removed the curtains from the window in my bedroom. As long as the sun shone, my phobia of the dark remained incognito. Once the sun set, my fear re-surfaced. Begging my big sister to spend the night in her room wasn't approved by mom. My unease for the dark hit me like a Texas-size tornado. Fearing someone might be watching me sleep gave me a whole lot of fright. Also, what if someone abducted me? Or what about the possibilities of lightning striking me? All these fears and more contaminated my mind. My mom said, "We live in the country and your bedroom is on the second floor. Abductors would have to climb a ladder to even get to your room." That did not re-assure me. My childish imagination continued to run wild.

"A homeless man could be out there staring at me," I responded. "My room is not safe!"

Changing mom's mind was not going to happen. I had a problem to solve and fast. The night was getting darker. My room was small with no extra space to rearrange the furniture. The only safe place from the window was directly underneath it.

Rearranging my pillows and bedspread, I curled up on the floor. That's where I slept until my curtains were hung up a week later. My worry was unending. Over the following few nights, I worried that someone would be outside looking in every time I entered my room.

My focus was on the unknown outside of my window. It wasn't until I prayed a couple of nights later that I started having a restful night. The lesson I want to emphasize is that prayer should have been my first and only action. There is no room for both worry and prayer.

"Be anxious for nothing, but in everything by prayer and supplication, with thanksgiving, let your requests be made known to God." Philippians 4:6

Time to share your lemonade:

I'm not a huge fan of the dark, however I'm not as scared as I used to be. What is a fear you have faced, and how did you overcome it?

Day 20

During the Autumn of my fourth-grade school year, mom and one of her friends decided it would be fun to take their two families camping. There was only one problem. My dad had handled all of the car troubles and dirty work that sometimes came along with camping. After he passed away, she had to do more on her own and often called for help. After considering the possibilities of what could go wrong, my mom and her friend agreed, "Maybe we should invite a handyman to come on our trip, too."

Luckily, my mom knew just the person to invite. This was the person my mom called every time she needed help around the house. We called him "Mr. Fix It." He knew about setting up tents, making sure our Winnebago was connected with water and building nice warm campfires. During the first evening, he led us out with singing and telling stories around a cozy fire. However, the evening turned to night, and we kids were encouraged to go to bed.

Climbing up into the bunk bed above the captain seat in the Winnebago, I fell fast asleep. About an hour into my deep slumber I heard a noise outside. Looking out of the window I saw the most unexpectedly frightful image, "Mr. Fix It" was kissing my mom goodnight. "Get away from my mother." I cried to myself.

Opening the door to the Winnebago, my mom heard me

crying. "What's wrong?" She asked me. "I need to go to the bathroom." I lied. I didn't have the courage to say, "I saw 'Mr. Fix It' kissing you." Permitting me to go use the restroom, I responded, "Never mind I don't need to go anymore."

The following morning I awoke to the aroma of pancakes frying on the grill. Instantly I found myself in a state of bathroom urgency. Tripping over my jeans, I struggled to pull them up and quickly get out the door. On the way to the outhouse, I unintentionally met up with "Mr. Fix It", "Are you going to marry my mother?" I blurted. I put him on the spot and created an extremely amusing awkward moment, that's for sure. He laughed and answered me with a sufficient response. Avoiding giving me pertinent information that my young age did not need to know, he responded with, "At this time I'm enjoying getting to know your mom." He remained confident and courageous in the presence of a confronting adolescent with a bold curiosity.

Kids love to ask questions, and that's ok. Communicating skills is vital to seeking out information. Thankfully 'Mr. Fix it' understood the emotion and intentions behind my question, and gave me a satisfactory answer. God gave him the wisdom to know how to handle opposition from an inquiring minor.

"Let your speech always be with grace, seasoned with salt, that you may know how you ought to answer each one." Colossians 4:6

Time to share your lemonade:

Tell of a memory when you were bold and asked for answers?

_____

_____

_____

_____

How was your question received?

_____

_____

_____

_____

Day 21

"Mr. Fix It" enjoyed getting to know my mom so much that he asked her to marry him. On November 28, 1977, our family grew, adding three more kids to the family roster. Care to guess who "Mr. Fix it" was? He was Richard Mitzelfelt, our former music teacher. He had two teenage daughters, Darla and Lynne. Remember, he also had a son named Monte? That "annoying boy" became my little brother. Isn't it funny how life takes an unexpected turn?

Monte was a picky eater. Getting him to eat healthy food was a constant battle for his dad. Mom joined in on the crusade, trying various tactics to encourage him to eat his food, but nothing worked. Meal times became a war zone. It was a constant fight between Monte and his vegetables.

On one occasion, Lynne arose to the challenge of personally getting him to eat carrots. She combined eggs, flour, sugar, vanilla, cinnamon, baking soda, and baking powder. Being a smart kid, Monte was pretty excited that she was making a cake and not anything gross like vegetables.

"I have one more ingredient to add before it's ready to be put in the oven," She announced as she dumped three cups of grated carrots in the mixture. "Don't worry," winking at him while pouring the batter into the cake pan. "There are no carrots in this one little section."

The sweet and spicy cake smelled delicious as Lynne

pulled it out of the oven. After cooling and then frosting it, she offered him a piece of flavorful moist carrot cake. Trusting his sister, Monte unknowingly gobbled up a serving size of carrots.

I love that God has a sense of humor. It's hysterical that Monte learned to enjoy his vegetables through eating cake. Even more hilarious is the fact he became my brother after I had so confidently announced my delight that he wasn't my brother.

The biggest lesson I have learned from my younger brother Monte is humility. In the beginning, the boy was challenging to me. I did not possess a gentle attitude toward him as a visitor in my home before he became my brother. Lynne, however, demonstrated a more humble approach on how to treat a challenging boy. Unlike both Lynne and me, Jesus is the ultimate example of humility. He did not value His self-importance or honor, but freely gave it up in every situation so that God would be glorified, even though it wasn't always easy.

Philippians 2:8, "And being found in appearance as a man, He humbled Himself and became obedient to the point of death, even the death of the cross.

Time to share your lemonade:

I believe God has a sense of humor. Unlike me, he is never cruel or vindictive. I love sharing my humbling story about being glad Monte wasn't my brother. Whether or not you are related to someone who annoys you, it is important to show kindness and patience.

What is a funny and humbling story that has happened to you?

_____

_____

_____

_____

_____

_____

_____

_____

Day 22

Playing baseball during summer vacation was a favorite activity of mine. My family didn't always have enough players for three bases, but running around two bases was equally fun. Spending the summer training with my family made me an unexpectedly skilled team player during the school year. The summer went by quickly. Lee and Lori went to a boarding school, hundreds of miles away in Loveland, Colorado. I went to school locally, not yet being in high school with my older siblings. Little did we know, our surroundings were about to change. My parents began searching for a new home for our big family. One problem... They forgot to tell Lee and Lori!

The feeling of when your parents pack up and move out of town without telling you, all while you're hundreds of miles away at a boarding school, is not a good one. It makes you feel afraid or even abandoned. Early in December of 1979, Lee and Lori temporarily lost contact with the rest of the family. Regularly every Friday night, they made phone calls home to check in with our parents.

Before cell phones, homes came equipped with landline telephones which were connected by wires to the wall. The dormitories at the academy only had payphones, a public telephone with a coin slot to pay before making a call. If the caller had no coins, there was an option to call collect, which means the receiver of the call would agree to pay for the charges. That's how Lee and Lori called home every week.

Imagine their shock when they called home, only to hear the operator say, "The number you dialed has been changed, disconnected, or is no longer in service. Please check the number and try again."

Feelings of abandonment and rejection plagued their minds. One traumatic week slipped away before they received word from their family that all was safe and sound. The family had moved to a new home in Placitas, NM. Lee and Lori realized that they had not, and would never be, abandoned. Yet, while they became more comfortable in their surroundings, I became less comfortable.

Entering a new school is tough, but in the middle of the school year, it's even harder. For the first time in my life, my disability became an easy target for teasing. The familiarity of my old friends in Farmington were a thing of the past. Fear arose inside me as I dreaded the first day at my new school. "Will the other students accept me?" I worried. During lunch on my first day of school, I heard a teasing voice blurt out.

"What happened to you? Why is your hand like this?" A girl called out to me, mocking me by holding her hand up with fingers curled in. Realizing the question was directed at me, I mumbled a reply, "I was in a car accident." Laughter filled the air as she walked away.

Every day at lunch, that same girl bullied me for looking a little different. Targeting me during recess, she taunted me to fight her. Name calling, judging, criticizing, and mocking me, she crushed my spirit. Holding-in my brokenness, I never told mom about the bully or her cohorts. Every night, I withdrew into my bedroom, dreading the next day. Those days of my life were a puddle of emotions, and my prayers for help seemed unanswered.

After one month at my new school, I was tired of being bullied. Enough was enough, I thought My courage and fearless attitude started to resurface. My confidence to stand up for myself grew like wildfire.

As luck would have it, we started playing baseball during P.E. This was my favorite sport, a game I had been playing with my family and friends for years, but none of my classmates took me seriously. Captains were chosen and they picked their team players. One by one, names were called to each side. My name was called last. Feeling somewhat defeated, I hung my head as I walked to my team's sideline. While sitting on the bench, my inner voice echoed, "Why are you upset? You've got this."

When it was my turn to bat I heard moans and groans from my teammates. "Great, she's an easy out. Get your gloves we'll be going to the field."

Refusing to allow those words to discourage me, I

proudly stood up to take my turn at bat. Breathing a deep sigh, I prayed, "Please, help me hit the ball." My confidence grew as I decided it was my time to shine. As God is my witness, I hit the ball and it soared where the birds fly, way above outfields reach. My team cheered for me as I made it to second base. Still, they didn't have faith in me quite yet.

Towards the end of the game, my team captain strategically devised a plan. "If the ball goes to Mary, let Tony try to catch it." My ego deflated hearing that remark. Why did I have to give up an opportunity? If I couldn't try catching it, then I didn't even want the ball to come my way.

As the batter stood at home plate, he looked directly my way. I knew what he was thinking; I'd miss the ball. Swinging his bat at the very first pitch, the ball ricocheted knee high in my direction. My guardian angels must have positioned my feet perfectly, because that ball wedged itself in between my knobby knees. I couldn't believe my eyes, or feel my knees for that matter. By the grace of God, I proved I don't even need one hand to catch the ball.

"Out," Yelled our teacher.

My team ran to me with hugs and high fives. Truly one of my most thrilling moments. My disability no longer defined my capability, and my classmates weren't laughing at me anymore.

The best way for me to stop the bullying was to be bigger than their teasing. I needed to show that they couldn't hurt me, and to put my best foot forward no matter what. By doing so, the bullying and teasing ultimately came to an end, and I actually became friends with my bully eventually.

It's not always possible or easy for people to face their bullies, though. Bullying is very serious and can be scary! Feelings of loneliness, abandonment or having no one to call upon are common to all of us. Even Jesus felt abandoned. In Matthew 27:46 he cried out, "My God, My God, Why have you forsaken me?" Yet, Jesus was not alone when he cried out those words. Always remember that God has not forsaken you, either. He is with you always.

If you are being bullied, here are a few ideas for how to deal with bullying. Don't isolate yourself; try to stay with other people. There's safety in numbers. Tell someone in authority to help you. If you feel safe, ask the bully to stop. Stand up tall and face the bully. Look the bully in the eye when you are speaking to them, keep your response short and direct, and say "Stop it." You can even let them know you'll report them if they don't stop. Remember to stay calm; the bully's goal is to get an emotional response from you.

If you witness bullying, here are a few ideas you can try to stand up for someone else. Take bullying seriously, it can escalate and cause serious damage. Get help right away. Be careful not to be part of group bullying by encouraging the bully with laughter. You can be brave by helping others!

Time to share your lemonade:

Never let anyone's opinion determine your capability. God might position your "feet" perfectly to stop the naysayers.

Write down a list of ways to be an encourager. If you have a story to share about beating the odds, please share that as well.

_____

_____

_____

_____

_____

_____

_____

_____

_____

Day 23

Have you ever wished to be a wallflower? A person with a timid personality who blends in without being noticed? I have. Standing in the background once sounded like the best idea to me because I didn't want people to notice that I am different. Can you think of something that blends? Choirs do! That's why I joined the choir in high school. A perfect class for not standing out.

At the beginning of my freshman year in high school, the choir director announced that we'd be voting for officers. "We will start with voting for the secretary position." A voice spoke up right away and said. "I nominate Mary." I was the first to be nominated!

"Wait, what? No, not me." I thought. "I'm a wallflower, I blend in." Other students were also nominated, which was good. The more nominees, the less likely for me to become the secretary.

As the nominees sat in a separate room waiting for the voting to be over, one of the other nominees made a prediction, "I bet Mary's going to get it." Shaking my head I thought, "No, not me. My job is to blend in."

The results were tallied and the verdict made. As we rejoined the choir, the announcement was made, "Mary is this year's choir secretary."

Thinking to myself and God, "Ok, Lord, I told you I'm

a wall-flower, why did you allow this to happen?" However, immediately after my questioning, I felt a peace in my heart, and the answer came to mind, "Maybe my focus should not be on blending in, but on being my best self."

From that moment on, I tried to change my attitude about myself. It wasn't easy, but after three years of high school, I had the confidence to run for senior class president. Imagine my delight as I told my mom, "I was voted as senior class president today!"

By the end of my senior year, while preparing for the class president's speech for graduation, I reflected back on my high school career. In the beginning, I tried not to be noticed by others, but throughout each year of high school I grew more confident in letting people see me.

Finally, the last day of my senior year, during commencement, I fearlessly stood up in front of hundreds of people and with confidence. I addressed my class and the audience with a heartfelt speech. Not only did I get up and speak, but also I agreed to sing a solo during the ceremony.

During my freshman year, I allowed my handicap to define me. I didn't want to be noticed as being different in high school. However, by the time I became a senior, I embraced my differences and was able to face my fears. God created me to be fearless. So, I would not allow for excuses to prevent me from being any other way.

"Let your light so shine before men, that they may see your good works and glorify your Father in heaven. Matthew 5:16

Time to share your lemonade:

What is something that might be preventing you from letting your light shine? How can you use that to inspire others?

_____

_____

_____

_____

_____

_____

Day 24

Before my dad had passed away, there was talk about possible amputation of my paralyzed arm. As a result, I flew all over the USA to meet with specialty doctors throughout my childhood. Each one of my doctors wanted to explore the possibility of a prosthetic arm. As a young child the concept of amputating my arm was terrifying. My mom didn't want to rush me into making a big and scary decision, especially after my dad died. So, she decided to let me wait until I turned 18 to make the choice.

During our travels, mom was my personal event planner. Every trip included a detailed itinerary of flight, doctor visits, hotels, eating, and outfits. Every appointment mom made sure I presented myself well. Representing the Shriners meant caring about my appearance.

Every one of my medical appointments consisted of examining my arm's range of movement and discriminating between sharp and dull objects. Trying to raise my paralyzed arm using only my shoulder muscles was impossible. Looking away from the doctor, while being prodded with a needle became annoying. Yes, I did feel the sharp prick, and it hurt.

Time passed, and I felt more and more nervous about amputation. With only one year until my 18th birthday, I still hadn't made a decision. Having concerns about my opinion of amputating, mom asked me how I felt about a prosthetic arm. She stated that dad had wanted me to go ahead with it, but that my input was all that mattered.

Criticizing my appearance and fearing I'd look more awkward without an arm, or with a fake arm, haunted me. My fear of what I might look like grew into a monster-like image, and I felt that if I looked like a monster I would feel less loved. Yet, what I didn't realize at that time is no one else saw me as a monster. Only I saw myself that way. All around me, people loved and supported me. That wouldn't change, no matter what I decided to do about my arm. After praying about it, my decision was simple, "Will I be bionic?"

"No." Mom responded.

"Then I don't want to amputate my arm."

After fourteen years living with a paralyzed arm, my decision not to amputate felt right. Welcoming myself to the world of adulthood by praying about a life-altering decision became my defining moment. Sure I was the girl with a paralyzed arm, but I was also the "fearless" girl with a paralyzed arm who was loved and supported by so many people.

"I sought the Lord, and He heard me, And delivered me from all my fears." Psalms 34:4

Time to share your lemonade:

When you have a tough decision to make, what do you like to do?

☐ *Seek advice from others.*

☐ *Make your own decision and then ask God to bless it.*

☐ *Seek the wisdom of God first.*

☐ _____

Share a time when you were faced with a tough decision. How did you approach it?

_____

_____

_____

_____

_____

Day 25

As children grow into adults, birthday gifts tend to get a lot more sophisticated. My eighteenth birthday was the pivotal year of ending all childish gifts. That was the year Ty and his wife Jennifer gave me a beautiful porcelain potpourri ornament to hang in my closet. What a grown-up gift!

Inside the ornament, white potpourri tablets resembling tiny pills emitted a lavender aroma. With that gift, my closet smelled like a dryer full of fresh clean clothes. Smelly shoes were a thing of the past! My closet could have been a flower garden to the blind. One morning as I tidied my room by throwing shoes and laundry in my closet, I heard mom call out to me, "When you get home from school, we need to talk."

Those are scary words coming from a mom. Various forms of the question, "Oh no, what did I do this time?" Haunted me all throughout the school day. I don't know of anyone who isn't scared of hearing their mom say, "We need to talk."

I usually liked it when my school day went by fast, but not this time. I truly wanted the day to slow down. I was praying for the day to never end, from my first period class, Bible, to my last period class, English. When the final class dismissal bell rang, I prolonged leaving school. Driving home, I drove 5 MPH under the speed limit. What kid does that? The kid who has a mom wanting to talk does. Perfectly obeying all the traffic rules, I became the best teenage driver in town. After supper, mom called me into the living room and told me to sit down. "I found something that concerns me." She paused. "I found an illegal substance in your closet. While I was in town this afternoon, I stopped by the pharmacist. He validated my suspicions. These are homemade drugs."

Reaching into her purse and pulling out little white pills from a plastic bag, she sternly asked, "Where did these come from?"

"Ty and Jennifer gave them to me," I said, trying hard not to laugh or be disrespectful. We sat staring at one another for what seemed like an eternity before I spoke again, "Mom, they're not drugs. Smell them."

I can't explain how lavender scented potpourri tricked my mom and her pharmacist, but I am thankful my mom had an intervention plan to stop her daughter from using illegal drugs. Abusing drugs has not been an issue for me, but mom didn't know my strong will power to say "No." She saw a potential problem and made plans to intervene no matter what the cost.

"Now no chastening seems to be joyful for the present, but painful; nevertheless, afterward it yields the peaceable fruit of righteousness to those who have been trained by it." Hebrews 11:12

Time to share your lemonade:

It was hard to be chastised in the moment, but it was ultimately a good thing. Thankfully it was a big misunderstanding. I realized then and there that my mom had my best interest at heart, and for that I am thankful.

How has a parent or role model intervened in your life?

_____

_____

_____

_____

_____

_____

_____

_____

Day 26

The Summer before I started ninth grade, my mom planned a trip, not a vacation but an outing to the Albuquerque Zoo. At that time, I was especially alert to my surroundings, or more accurately, I was alert to any cute guys around me. Too shy to flirt, I still cared about my appearance. I also really cared about NOT being seen with my pesky little brothers.

The Albuquerque Zoo had animal exhibits representing countries from all over the world: Birds of America, Australian Outback, Polar Bears, and Apes are a few of the habitats we visited. However, after this particular trip, the exhibit I will never forget was the African Lions.

As we were touring the zoo, minding our own business, along came two cute guys, maybe high school seniors if I had to guess. Noticing that they seemed to be walking in the same direction as us, I glanced at my reflection in a glass enclosure to see how I looked. My hair was freshly combed, my shirt was correctly buttoned, and there was nothing clinging to my teeth. Everything checked out, so I held my head high and tried to act casually cool.

"Aren't we here to look at the *animals*?" My little brother Daren asked, when he noticed me eyeing the boys.

I ignored my brother. I still needed to keep up appearances. Hoping to look more mature, I pulled my shoulders back and held my head up high. I was so focused on how I looked that I hardly even noticed the animals.

Entering the African Lions' exhibit, Daren read the sign above the walkway, "Caution: Area Under Construction." Only two things protected us from the lions, a deep trench and a stainless steel cable netting. The lion was only five feet away. I'm sure we could have felt the lion's hot breath if he had roared! Instead, something much worse happened.

Picking up his hind legs, the lion pointed a stream of pee right at me. There was no time to dodge the misfortune. All my earlier concerns of looking proper were in vain. Suddenly, I was noticed. This was not the kind of attention I wanted! Drenched with lion pee as my little brothers pointed and laughed, I was a spectacle. This was not part of the plan to get noticed, but it happened. Perhaps if I had paid more attention to my surroundings than to my pride, things might have turned out much differently.

Proverbs 11:2 says, "When pride comes, then comes shame; But with the humble is wisdom."

Time to share your lemonade:

Being peed on by a lion is a feat I bet not many people have experienced. The incident was humbling and, in hindsight, is now hilarious. It makes me remember that if we stay humble, honouring God, pride will have a hard time getting into our hearts.

How have you kept humble when you were tempted to be prideful?

Day 27

On my fifteenth birthday I received a plain white ordinary envelope from my mom. My puzzled expression said it all. Is this a last-minute gift? Are there too many kids in the family for you and Richard to remember everyone's birthday? Opening the envelope, a piece of paper fell out. There on the floor lay a certificate for drivers ed. It was the best birthday gift I could ever have imagined. It was the beginning of my freedom. My enthusiasm for receiving this amazing white extraordinary envelope showed through my dancing and hugs.

After weeks of classroom studies and months of behind the wheel practice, I finally earned my license. Independence at last! Except for a couple of rules my parents had for me. I was only allowed to drive to school and back home, or else I would suffer severe consequences. The first car I was permitted to drive was an olive green 1973, Oldsmobile, Delta 88. The car was as large as a luxurious passenger ship. While behind the wheel, I felt like the captain of the SS Delta cruise ship. The ride was smooth sailing. One nice benefit of driving a large car was that the weight of it kept me on the snow-packed roads during the winter. A disadvantage was that the car's year and model was prehistoric and certainly did not have backup cameras. There were terrible blind spots on all sides of the vehicle. Especially the back end of the car.

The summer after I got my driver's license I worked as an assistant to the registrar at the private high school I attended. During summer the campus was used for camp meeting. I worked at the school, and my job duties included greeting visitors, answering phones, and running errands. In New Mexico, the summer heat often hit triple digits. During those hot days I didn't enjoy walking from one end of the campus to the other. Making the decision to break the rules, I decided to drive my car on my errands instead of walking in the terrible heat. Not a big deal. There was no traffic. I stayed on campus, and I thought all that driving also provided great parking practice. After driving back and forth several times, I became more confident with my driving ability. My overconfidence in my driving led to carelessness. At the end of the day, zipping out of my parking spot, I bumped into something. Not seeing anything in my rearview mirror, I left the scene.

The first thing the following morning, a police officer entered the registrar's office, not the kind of person I expected to greet at camp meeting, "Who owns the Delta 88 parked in front of the administration building?"
Gulp, "Huh, my parents." There was a pause, "But I drive it."

"Did you back into anything yesterday afternoon?"
I wanted to cry! Instead I quietly said, "Yes, sir."

The officer let me know that I had hit a parked car. What a humbling experience. I loved driving from one end of campus to the other end. "Freely" hopping in the car to run errands created a sense of independence. However, along with having a driver's license, there's also a responsibility of driving safely and obeying laws. Because I did not obey the "law," I was grounded.

*"This Book of the Law shall not depart from your mouth, but you shall meditate in it day and night, that you may observe to do according to all that is written in it. For then you will make your way prosperous, and then you will have good success."
Joshua 1:8*

Time to share your lemonade:

Freedom is the ability to make decisions. Responsibility is being held accountable for your actions. When I got my driver's license I had the freedom to decide when and where I could drive, but I was held accountable for my actions after I broke my parents rules.

Describe a situation when you made a mistake and felt the consequences.

_____

_____

_____

_____

Day 28

A career as a chef was never a consideration for me. However, my mom had this crazy notion that I needed to learn about and know how to use all the equipment found in a kitchen. For example: oven, stove, refrigerator, and of course the dishwasher. "What's your poor husband going to do if you don't know your way around the kitchen?" She teased me.

"I don't believe the kitchen is just for women," I said. "If my husband gets hungry, he can make something for himself and me." Since mom had authority over me, she ordered me to help prepare dinner. "You're going to make cornbread for supper tonight." She commanded. Handing me the recipe, she let me fend for myself. "Besides, husband or not, you need to learn how to cook."

Glancing at the list of ingredients, I mischievously decided, "I have a better recipe." Instantly my baking extravaganza began. As a joke, I reached for a bag of frozen corn from the freezer and a loaf of bread from the cabinet.

Mom looked at me most pecurally as she questioned my cooking methods. "What on earth are you doing?"

"I'm making cornbread! Corn. And Bread."

Hoping she would give up on her fanciful idea of me cooking didn't go as planned. Mom reviewed the recipe step by step with me. Her instructions also include a lot more than just opening a package of premixed cornbread and adding milk and eggs. I had to *actually* measure things. Searching for the ingredients was like a game of hide-and-go-seek. I couldn't find anything, and I wanted to give up. "Olly olly oxen free," I called, but no food came out of hiding.

Grudgingly, I found all the ingredients and dumped them together in a bowl. Retrieving the electric mixer, I blended the contents until the batter was smooth. No complications arose when I poured the mixture into a baking dish, and placed it in the oven. Thirty minutes later, my cornbread was golden brown. It looked amazing.

As we sat around the table, mom prayed. "Bless this food and the hands that prepared it." As soon as she said *Amen*, everyone dug into the food. Mom was the first to taste my cornbread, and she was the first to spit it out. Before I knew it, everyone was spitting cornbread out. Seeing my family's reaction, I wasn't even brave enough to taste it.

"What did you put in this cornbread?! Did you follow the directions I gave you?" My mom asked, taking a big drink of water to wash down the nasty taste.

Getting up to show her all the ingredients I used, I repeated, "Cornmeal, eggs, baking soda, milk, and butter."

"Baking soda?" she wailed. "The ingredients said to use baking powder." Honestly, I didn't know there was a difference between baking powder and baking soda. Thinking both were the same product, I had grabbed the baking soda.

Through this experience, I learned that it's important

to know the difference between baking powder and baking soda. Even though they both start with "baking" they respond differently to ingredients. My mom decided baking may not be my forte. My family agreed if I'm preparing dinner, everyone should pray prior to baking. What we all were thinking was, "Thank God for the gift of mom's cooking."

Exodus 35:10 "All who are gifted artisans among you shall come and make all that the Lord has commanded."

Time to share your lemonade:

Obviously my talent isn't baking cornbread. I am good at other things, though. For example, I'm good at encouraging my friends when they're feeling down.

Write about one of your talents or skills that you're proud of.

_____

_____

_____

_____

Day 29

The car I drove in high school was a 1974 Dodge Dart. The car was built with a carburetor that mixes gasoline and air together, creating a spark to make it start. Many mornings "The Dart" refused to start. Richard taught me an alternate way to start the car by feeding it with gasoline through the carburetor.

Another quirky characteristic of the car was that it had a terrible green color. Honestly, I believed my parents had a private meeting to discuss the ugliest car they would buy. The color, size and unique starting strategy all played into their ugliest car plan. Although, their claim to buying it was for "safety."

One particular morning, I had an early appointment with one of my teachers. Only giving myself enough wiggle room to get dressed, eat and leave, I panicked when my car refused to start. Opening the hood and popping off the carburetor gap, I fed it fuel. After a few cranks It finally revved up.

That's when I noticed white flakes falling from the sky. Snow fell during the night covering our driveway and the road leading to the main street. Time was of the essence. Inching my way down the windy steep hill, my tires lost traction after hitting an ice patch. The Dart lost control, fishtailing down the curvy slope. It slid off the road and leaped over a ditch into a ravine. My car was stuck.

The Dart didn't dodge misfortune. "DEADLINE" was on my mind, and I couldn't be late. Putting the car in drive and then reverse, and repeating somehow got me back on the road again. However, the car kept pulling to the left, so I turned the steering wheel to the right. Maneuvering the Dart all the way up the hill to home was a miracle. Opening the car door, I slowly made my way into the house. "Mom, we have a problem," I said.

Assessing the car, Richard came back inside looking perplexed, "How did you manage to drive the car home? The axle is broken."

One word, "Angels."

"For He shall give His angels charge over you, to keep you in all your ways." Psalms 91:11

Time to share your lemonade:

Reflect on a memory when looking back you thought, "Angels were protecting me." Share how God sent His angels to protect you along the road.

_____

_____

Write a thank you to God for protecting and helping you.

Day 30

"When life gives you lemons, make lemonade." This is a simple yet powerful message. Lemons represent our problems, and lemonade represents our solutions to problems. My "lemon" is having only one hand. There are seemingly simple things that I struggle with, such as tying shoes, clapping, swimming, typing, or even putting my hair in a ponytail. Making lemonade for me is learning how to do those things independently.

My parents taught me to focus on solutions, not problems. To be honest solving problems hasn't always been easy for me. Sometimes I need friends to help figure things out. They give me a different perspective on the problem. While having a conversation with my friend Terry, I mention wanting to learn to kayak. However, a kayaker needs two hands to paddle the boat. Terry came up with an idea, "We'll connect a rope from my kayak to your kayak. You can still paddle but I'll do most of the work."

Words cannot express the emotions of my first kayaking trip. Grinning from ear to ear, tears rolling down my cheeks, and a heart overflowing with gratitude while I sat in the kayak for the very first time. Connected by a rope, we paddled side by side on my first kayaking adventure. My forearm pressed flat on the paddle while controlling it as I maneuvered it from one side of the kayak to the other, when my arm grew weary from paddling, Terry towed me.

Perhaps the best thing about that kayaking trip was how we traveled peacefully across the water. Turtles popped their heads up to say, "Hello!" Cranes flew over our heads directing us where to go and a cool breeze pushed us forward. I didn't have Terry's strength, but I was accomplishing something I didn't think possible. Through his idea of helping me kayak, we both were making lemonade.

There are days I get discouraged trying to figure things out. Sometimes I cry with frustration, not being able to do things most people take for granted, like buckling a watch band. God has given me the determination to conquer obstacles, though. And yes, I have now learned to clasp my watch band!

When I get to heaven there are many things I want to do with two hands. I'm looking forward to clapping, water skiing on the sea of glass, playing any string instrument, cartwheels and flips, the list goes on, but at the very top I'm looking forward to wrapping both arms around my dad. Until that day, I will be setting up my lemonade stand and sharing my story with anyone who will listen.

"And we know that all things work together for good to those who love God, to those who are called according to His purpose." Romans 8:28

Journal Pages

Take time over the next few days to think about your story that God is working with you to write. These final pages are here for you to write about both the good and bad things that you have experienced. Look for God's love in every circumstance. Once you've written your story, I hope you find the courage and strength to share it with the world.

Mary's Lemonade Recipe

Ingredients

8 Lemons (aka your problem)
1 cup of Sugar (sweetens the burden and makes it less gruesome)
8 Cups of Water (waters down and removes the bitterness)

Instructions

Wash the lemons, cut into slices and place in a large bowl, add sugar. Mash the lemons and sugar until blended together, 2 minutes. Strain the juice (about 2 cups) and combine it to 8 cups of water in a pitcher. Best served cold and with a friend.

About the Author

Mary Rudisaile is a first-time author living in Granbury, Texas. Through sharing her story, Mary hopes to show that overcoming obstacles is possible with a can-do spirit. Mary is a mother to two grown girls that she is very proud of. Now that she's put a checkmark in front of "write a book" on her bucket list, she is excited to start checking even more items off her list. These include learning to water ski, taking a hot-air balloon ride, hiking Machu Picchu, learning how to knit, and continuing to tell her story.

Made in the USA
Middletown, DE
10 January 2022